Creative Education

DINOSAURS

On The Cover:
Tyrannosaurus rex.
Dinosaurs like this "ruled the earth"
for more than 130 million years.
Cover Art by Walter Stuart.

Published by Creative Education, Inc., 123 South Broad Street, Mankato, Minnesota 56001

Printed by permission of Wildlife Education, Ltd.

ISBN 0-88682-393-5

Created and written by
John Bonnett Wexo

Chief Artist
Walter Stuart

Senior Art Consultant
Mark Hallett

Design Consultant
Eldon Paul Slick

Production Art Director
Maurene Mongan

Production Artists
Bob Meyer
Fiona King
Hildago Ruiz

Photo Staff
Renee C. Burch
Katharine Boskoff

Publisher
Kenneth Kitson

Associate Publisher
Ray W. Ehlers

DINOSAURS

This Volume is Dedicated to: Charles Robbins Schroeder, a great man and steadfast friend. Without his guidance and wisdom, Zoobooks would never have existed.

Art Credits

Page Eight: Lower Left, John Sibbick; Upper Right, Robert Bampton; Pages Eight and Nine: John Sibbick; Page Nine: Upper Right, Walter Stuart; Page Ten: Upper Right, Robert Bampton; Middle, John Sibbick; Lower Left, Walter Stuart; Page Eleven: Left, John Sibbick; Upper Right, Walter Stuart; Middle Right and Lower Right, Robert Bampton; Page Twelve: Upper Right, Walter Stuart; Upper Middle and Lower Left, John Sibbick; Lower Middle, Robert Bampton; Pages Twelve and Thirteen: Center, John Sibbick; Page Thirteen: Upper Right and Lower Right, John Sibbick; Upper Middle and Lower Left, Robert Bampton; Page Fourteen: John Sibbick; Page Fifteen: Upper Left, Walter Stuart; Right and Bottom, John Sibbick; Page Sixteen: Upper Right and Lower Right, Walter Stuart; Pages Sixteen and Seventeen: John Sibbick; Page Eighteen: Lower Left, Robert Bampton; Pages Eighteen and Nineteen: John Sibbick; Page Nineteen: Upper Left and Right, Walter Stuart; Middle Right, Walter Stuart; Page Twenty: Middle Left, Walter Stuart; Lower Left, Robert Bampton; Pages Twenty and Twenty-one: John Sibbick; Page Twenty-one: Middle Right, Walter Stuart; Pages Twenty-two and Twenty-three: Background, Timothy Hayward; Figures, Chuck Byron.

Photographic Credits

Pages Six and Seven: Gordon Menzie (Models by Tyrrell Museum of Paleontology and Walter Stuart); Page Eight: Middle Left, Menzie Photography (Carina Schoening); Middle Right, Lower Middle and Lower Right, Gordon Menzie (Models by Bill Lightner); Page Nine: Upper Left, Gordon Menzie; Page Eleven: Lower Middle and Middle Right, J. D. Stewart (Los Angeles County Museum); Page Fifteen: Middle Left, Mitch Reardon (Photo Researchers).

Creative Education would like to thank Wildlife Education, Ltd., for granting them the right to print and distribute this hardbound edition.

Contents

Dinosaurs _____ 6-7

Dinosaurs were different _____ 8-9

Meat-eating dinosaurs _____ 10-11

Armor was important _____ 12-13

The biggest dinosaurs _____ 14-15

Long necks _____ 16-17

Reptile giants ruled the oceans _____ 18-19

The end of the dinosaurs _____ 20-21

Remember _____ 22-23

Index _____ 24

They sure were BIG . . .

BOOK SEVEN

Dinosaurs

The most wonderful reptiles of all began to evolve about 225 million years ago—the amazing dinosaurs. As you have seen, the dinosaurs were descended from an earlier reptile group, the thecodonts. But the dinosaurs were **much more successful** than the thecodonts. They filled many niches and "took over the world." And they continued to be the "rulers" of the world for more than **130 million years**—a period that is known as **the Age of Dinosaurs.** During that time, there were many different kinds of dinosaurs. Some grew very large, to become **the largest** land animals that have ever lived. Others became **the most ferocious predators** that have ever lived. Why did the dinosaurs become so successful? Why did some of them grow so big? And why did they suddenly die out? Let's take a look . . .

Dinosaurs were different from other animals, and that was the main reason why they were able to take over the world. As a group, they were better at **finding food** and **protecting themselves** than any animals that had ever lived on land.

Meat-eating dinosaurs could run faster and catch more prey than any other meat-eating animals. And plant-eating dinosaurs were better at finding plants and protecting themselves from predators than other plant-eating animals.

Dinosaurs were able to do all of these things because they were descended from a remarkable group of reptiles called **the thecodonts**. Dinosaurs inherited several valuable things from thecodonts.

ARMOR

ORNITHOSUCHUS

Some dinosaur ancestors had **small pieces of bone** in the skin on their backs. As dinosaurs evolved, these bones grew larger in some kinds of dinosaurs, and finally became **heavy armor** on some of them.

LONG TAILS

Like some thecodonts, many dinosaurs could stand up on two feet. They had long tails that **balanced the weight** of their bodies over their legs—like a seesaw balancing.

STRONGER LEGS

Whether they walked on two legs or four legs, all dinosaurs had their legs **under** their bodies. This made the legs stronger, so they could support more weight—and it made it easier for dinosaurs **to run.**

To help them balance on two legs, many dinosaurs had **long toes.** The toes could be spread out to provide greater stability for the foot—in the same way that **a tripod** gives solid support for a camera.

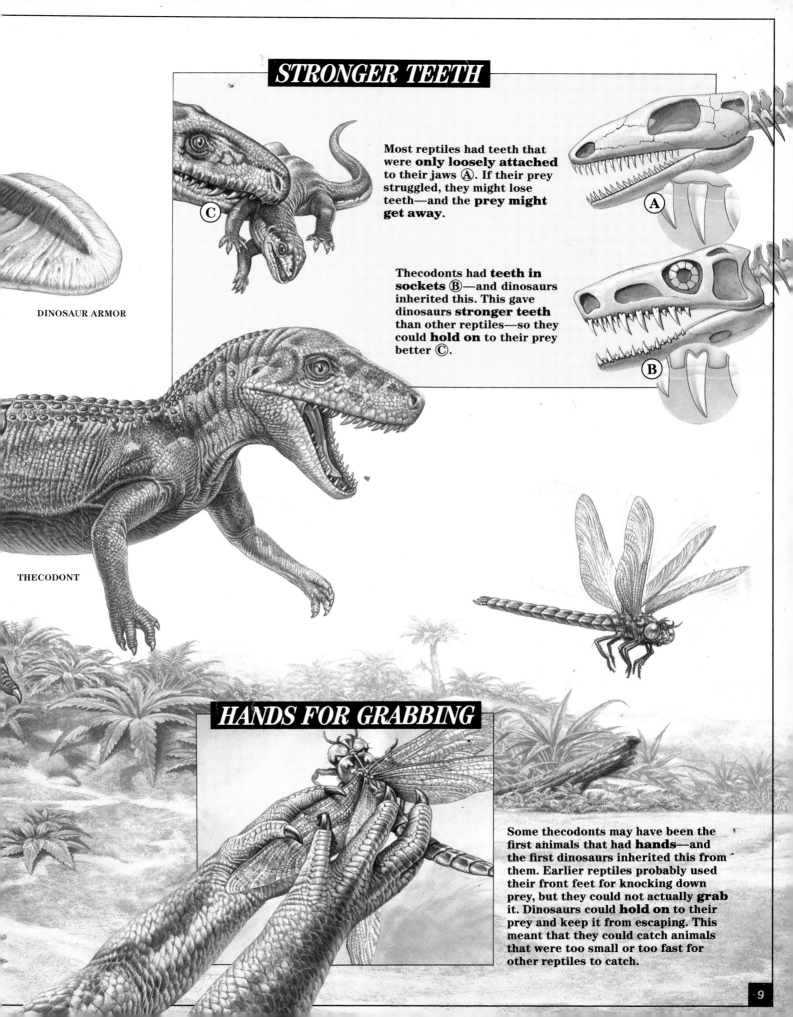

STRONGER TEETH

Most reptiles had teeth that were **only loosely attached** to their jaws Ⓐ. If their prey struggled, they might lose teeth—and the **prey might get away.**

Thecodonts had **teeth in sockets** Ⓑ—and dinosaurs inherited this. This gave dinosaurs **stronger teeth** than other reptiles—so they could **hold on** to their prey better Ⓒ.

DINOSAUR ARMOR

THECODONT

HANDS FOR GRABBING

Some thecodonts may have been the first animals that had **hands**—and the first dinosaurs inherited this from them. Earlier reptiles probably used their front feet for knocking down prey, but they could not actually **grab** it. Dinosaurs could **hold on** to their prey and keep it from escaping. This meant that they could catch animals that were too small or too fast for other reptiles to catch.

DROMAEOSAURUS

HYPACROSAURUS

Meat-eating dinosaurs were like their thecodont ancestors in many ways. All of them had
long back legs and shorter front legs. Many
had hands. And all of them had large mouths, with
many sharp teeth that were held tightly in sockets.

As time passed, however, meat-eating dinosaurs
evolved in ways that made them **much better** at catching prey than thecodonts had ever been. The back
legs on the dinosaurs became longer and stronger. In
general, their heads and jaws became larger—and their
teeth got bigger, too. In the end, meat-eating dinosaurs
developed into **the most terrible animals** that have ever
lived on earth.

The main prey of meat-eating
dinosaurs was plant-eating
dinosaurs. **Like lions or
wolves** today, smaller meat-
eaters may have **hunted in
packs** and killed plant-eaters
that were much larger than
they were.

LONG LEGS

There were meat-eating dinosaurs of
many different sizes, and they hunted
prey of many different sizes. But regard-
less of their size, almost all carnivorous
dinosaurs **ran on two legs** when they
chased their prey—because they had to
run faster than their prey.

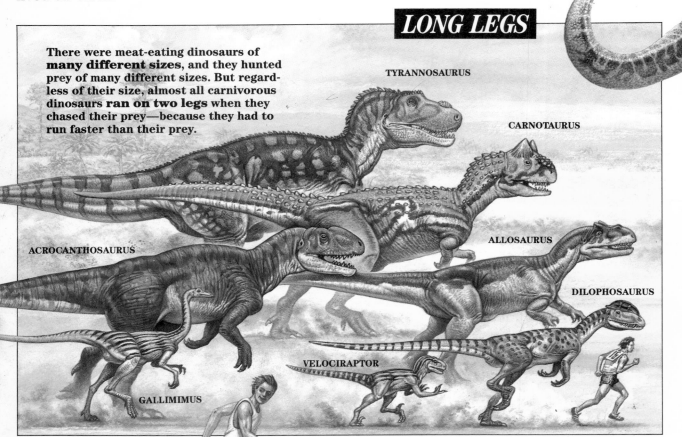

TYRANNOSAURUS

CARNOTAURUS

ACROCANTHOSAURUS

ALLOSAURUS

DILOPHOSAURUS

VELOCIRAPTOR

GALLIMIMUS

It's easy to see why longer legs can make you
run faster. With longer legs, every step you
take carries you further across the ground.
If you had legs that were **twice as long** as
everybody else, each step would take you
twice as far—and you would run **twice as
fast.** Some meat-eating dinosaurs could run
very fast—up to **40 miles per hour!**

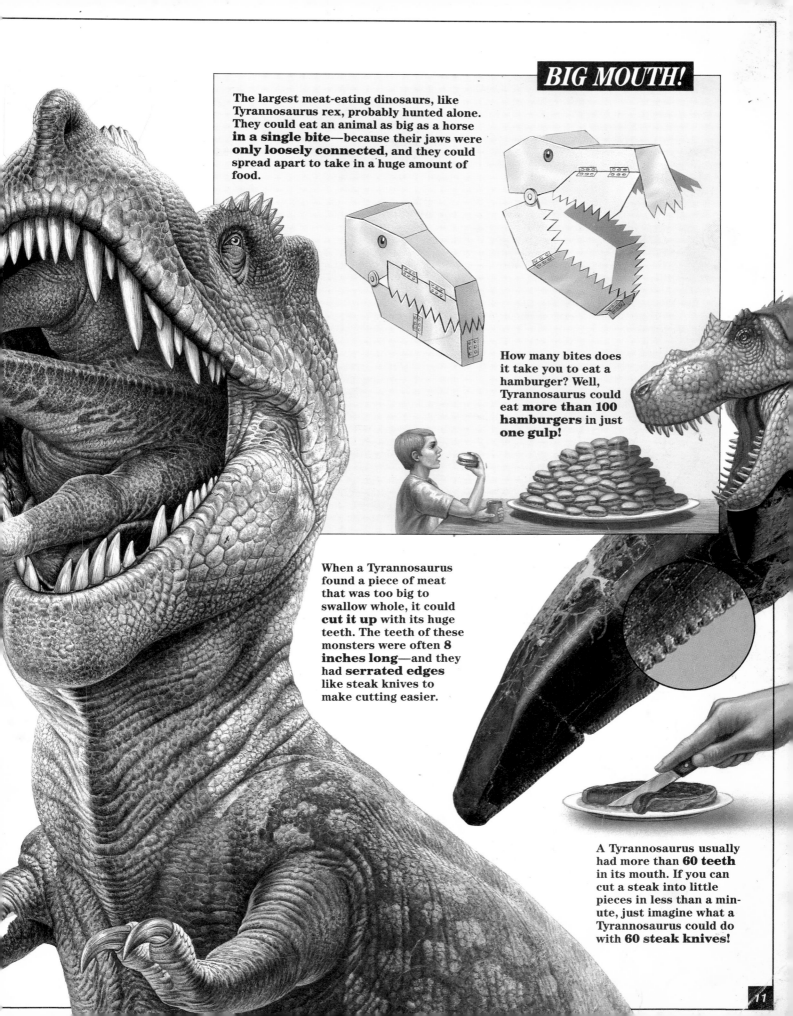

The largest meat-eating dinosaurs, like Tyrannosaurus rex, probably hunted alone. They could eat an animal as big as a horse **in a single bite**—because their jaws were **only loosely connected**, and they could spread apart to take in a huge amount of food.

How many bites does it take you to eat a hamburger? Well, Tyrannosaurus could eat **more than 100 hamburgers** in just **one gulp!**

When a Tyrannosaurus found a piece of meat that was too big to swallow whole, it could **cut it up** with its huge teeth. The teeth of these monsters were often **8 inches long**—and they had **serrated edges** like steak knives to make cutting easier.

A Tyrannosaurus usually had more than **60 teeth** in its mouth. If you can cut a steak into little pieces in less than a minute, just imagine what a Tyrannosaurus could do with **60 steak knives!**

Armor was important to many plant-eating dinosaurs, for obvious reasons. It helped to protect them from meat-eating dinosaurs.

The most heavily armored dinosaurs were the **ankylosaurs** (ann-KY-luh-sawrs). They had spikes and bony bumps covering the tops of their heads and their backs. **Stegosaurs** (STEG-uh-sawrs) were less heavily armored, with rows of bony plates down their backs. And **ceratopsians** (ser-uh-TOP-see-uns) had armor on their heads only.

Plant-eating dinosaurs had **very small brains** for the size of their bodies. Stegosaurus was 32 feet long, and weighed up to 6,000 pounds—but its brain was about the same size as **the brain of a cat**. Can you find the brain of Stegosaurus in the picture?

DASPLETOSAURUS

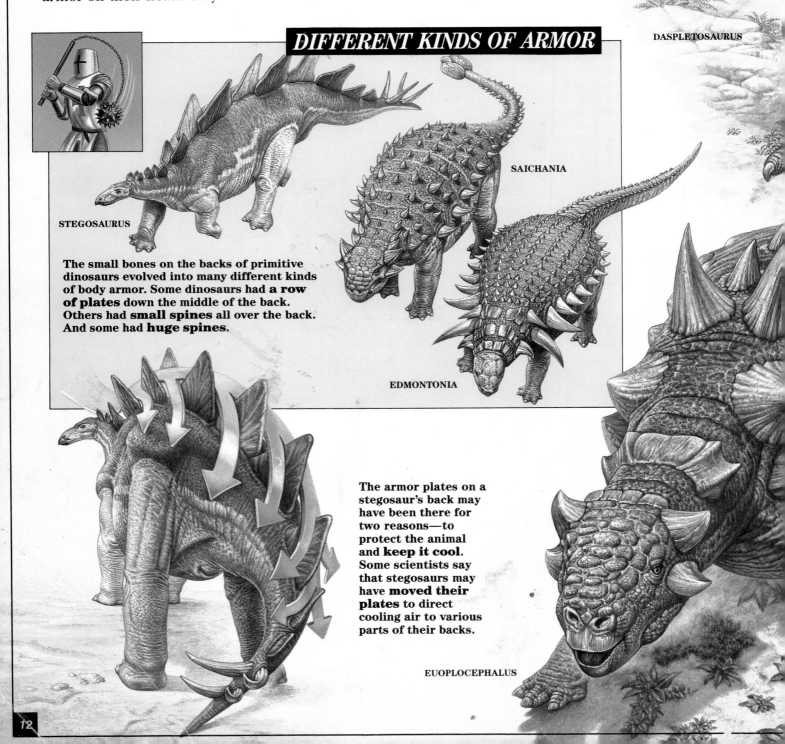

DIFFERENT KINDS OF ARMOR

STEGOSAURUS

SAICHANIA

EDMONTONIA

EUOPLOCEPHALUS

The small bones on the backs of primitive dinosaurs evolved into many different kinds of body armor. Some dinosaurs had **a row of plates** down the middle of the back. Others had **small spines** all over the back. And some had **huge spines**.

The armor plates on a stegosaur's back may have been there for two reasons—to protect the animal and **keep it cool**. Some scientists say that stegosaurs may have **moved their plates** to direct cooling air to various parts of their backs.

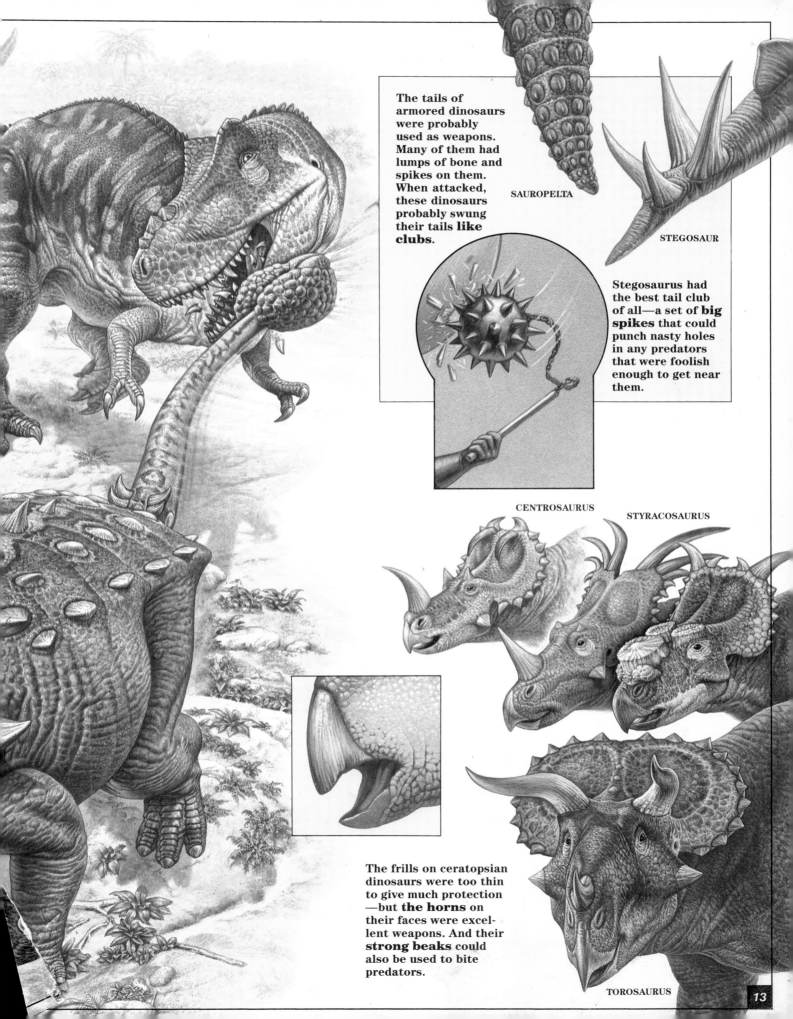

SAUROPELTA

STEGOSAUR

The tails of armored dinosaurs were probably used as weapons. Many of them had lumps of bone and spikes on them. When attacked, these dinosaurs probably swung their tails **like clubs**.

Stegosaurus had the best tail club of all—a set of **big spikes** that could punch nasty holes in any predators that were foolish enough to get near them.

CENTROSAURUS

STYRACOSAURUS

The frills on ceratopsian dinosaurs were too thin to give much protection —but **the horns** on their faces were excellent weapons. And their **strong beaks** could also be used to bite predators.

TOROSAURUS

The biggest dinosaurs were plant-eaters called **sauropods** (SORE-uh-podz). These huge animals walked on four legs and did not move very fast. They had **very long necks and long tails**.

Why were sauropods **so big**? There are several possible reasons. One has to do with **the food they ate**. As you know, plant-eaters need bigger bodies to hold their bulky food. Or sauropods might have grown large so they could **stay warm and active** at night. As you will see, the bodies of larger reptiles can hold heat longer than smaller reptiles.

But the most likely reason is **protection from predators**. Large animals are less likely to be attacked—and when they are, they can use their great size to chase predators away.

YOUNG APATOSAURUS

A larger body holds heat longer than a small one. For this reason, dinosaurs could have grown bigger so they could stay warm and active for a longer time every day. During the warm part of the day, a big body **could absorb more heat** from the sun . . .

Then, when the sun went down and the air became colder, the big dinosaur body would have **more heat inside** than the bodies of smaller reptiles. So big dinosaurs could **keep moving after dark** —while smaller reptiles would lose heat more quickly, and be forced to stop moving.

Perhaps the best reason for being big is **protection**. A very big animal is less likely to be attacked by predators. Today, the largest land animal is the elephant, and no animal in the wild dares to attack a grown elephant.

DOWN ON 4 LEGS

EARLY DINOSAUR

The ancestors of sauropods probably walked on two legs most of the time, like meat-eating dinosaurs did. And early sauropods weren't very big.

CAMARASAURUS

As sauropods got larger and larger, it was harder and harder to balance on two legs. They began to spend more time standing on four legs.

DIPLODOCUS

Finally, the largest dinosaurs were **too heavy** to be supported by two legs. They spent almost all of their time on four legs.

SUPERSAURUS

The very largest sauropods were **the biggest and heaviest** land animals that ever lived. The giant Supersaurus was over 30 feet tall—and it weighed up to **100 thousand pounds**. That's as much as **40 compact cars!**

ALLOSAURUS

Long necks did the same thing for plant-eating sauropods that long necks do for giraffes. They made it easier for the dinosaurs **to reach their food.** Of course, the necks of sauropods were much longer than giraffe necks. An average giraffe neck is about 8 feet long—but the necks of the largest sauropods may have been more than **30 feet long.**

Like giraffes, sauropods ate leaves from trees. And their long necks made it possible for them to eat leaves that were **very high up.**

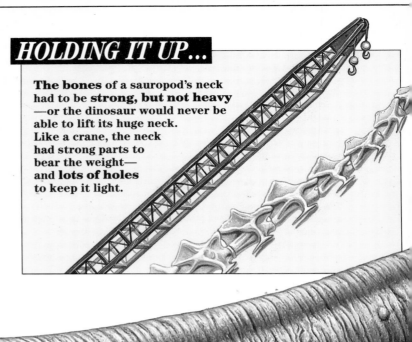

The bones of a sauropod's neck had to be **strong, but not heavy** —or the dinosaur would never be able to lift its huge neck. Like a crane, the neck had strong parts to bear the weight— and **lots of holes** to keep it light.

Remember that sauropods were descended from animals that walked on two feet. For this reason, even the largest sauropods had **longer and stronger legs in back** than in front. And when they wanted to, they could probably **rear up** on their back legs to reach leaves in very tall trees.

...AND MOVING IT

A crane is moved up and down by **a cable Ⓐ**. When the cable is pulled back **Ⓑ**, the crane moves up **Ⓒ**.

Sauropods had **strong ligaments** **Ⓓ** in their necks that worked like the cable on a crane. Many muscles could tighten the ligaments **Ⓔ** to pull the neck up **Ⓕ**.

DIPLODOCUS

MAMENCHISAURUS

BRACHIOSAURUS

LEAF EATING

After their long necks raised their heads up to the tree tops, sauropods had **different ways to eat** different kinds of leaves.

Some sauropods had small, stubby teeth. They may have **raked leaves** off branches. Others had sharp teeth that probably **clipped leaves** like garden shears.

SALTASAURUS

Like all dinosaurs, sauropods had long tails to help **balance the weight** of their long necks. The tails were also used as **weapons**.

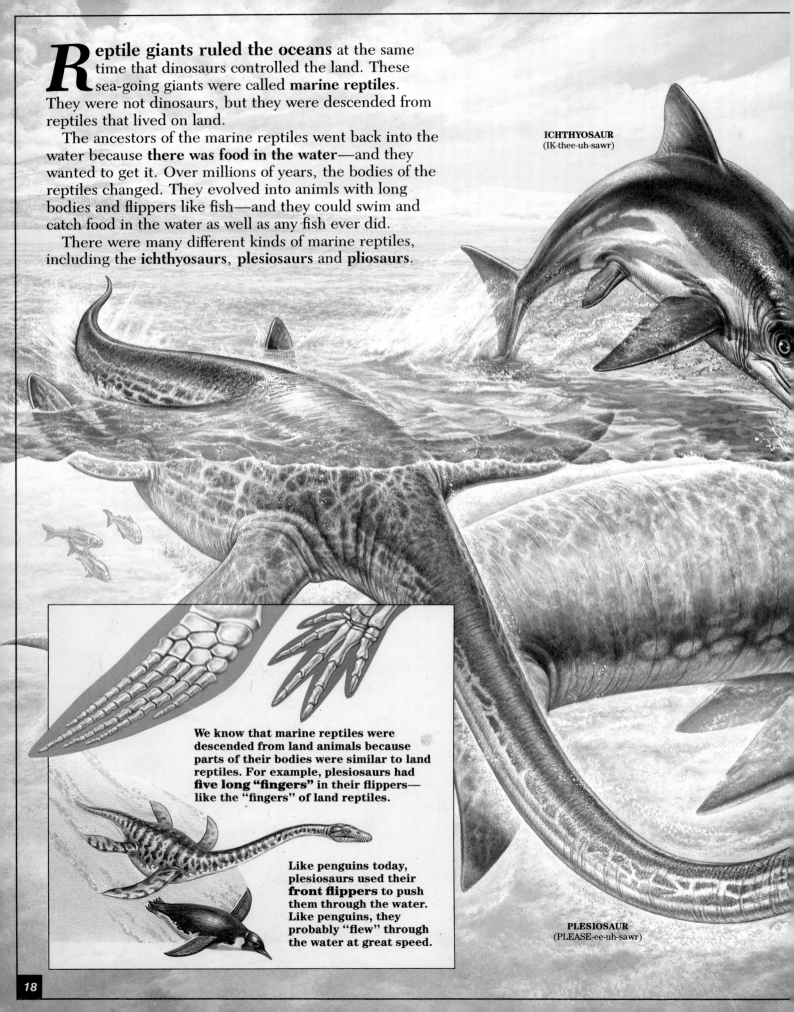

Reptile giants ruled the oceans at the same time that dinosaurs controlled the land. These sea-going giants were called **marine reptiles**. They were not dinosaurs, but they were descended from reptiles that lived on land.

The ancestors of the marine reptiles went back into the water because **there was food in the water**—and they wanted to get it. Over millions of years, the bodies of the reptiles changed. They evolved into animls with long bodies and flippers like fish—and they could swim and catch food in the water as well as any fish ever did.

There were many different kinds of marine reptiles, including the **ichthyosaurs**, **plesiosaurs** and **pliosaurs**.

ICHTHYOSAUR
(IK-thee-uh-sawr)

We know that marine reptiles were descended from land animals because parts of their bodies were similar to land reptiles. For example, plesiosaurs had **five long "fingers"** in their flippers— like the "fingers" of land reptiles.

Like penguins today, plesiosaurs used their **front flippers** to push them through the water. Like penguins, they probably "flew" through the water at great speed.

PLESIOSAUR
(PLEASE-ee-uh-sawr)

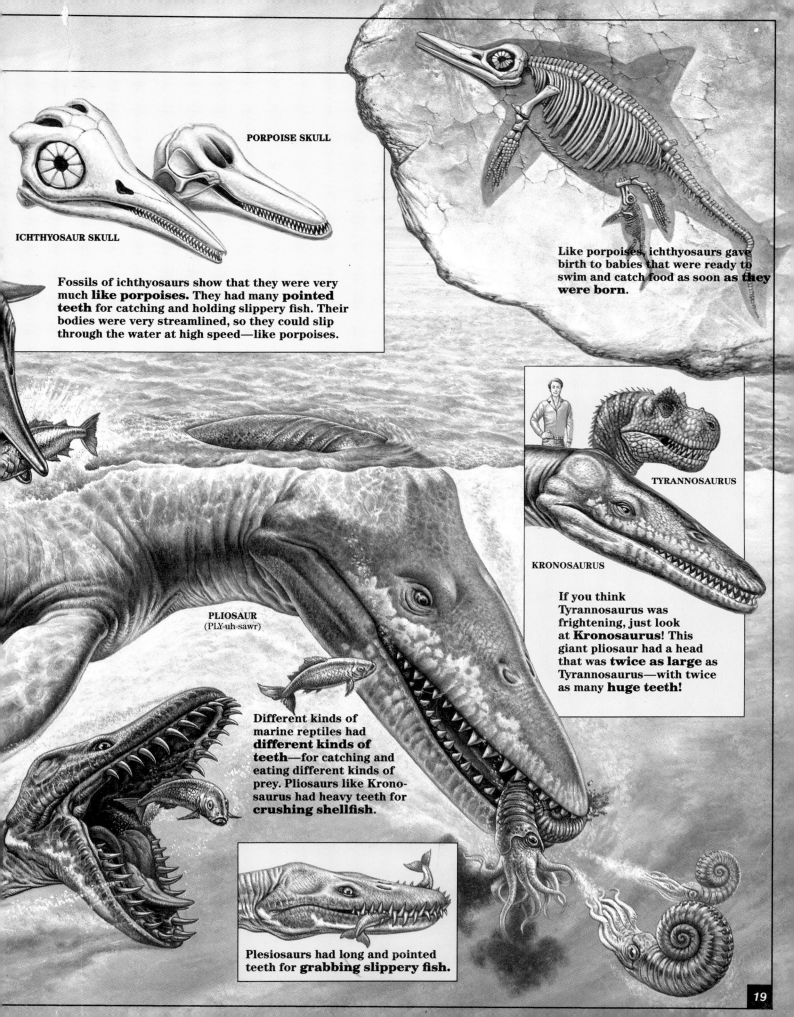

PORPOISE SKULL

ICHTHYOSAUR SKULL

Fossils of ichthyosaurs show that they were very much **like porpoises.** They had many **pointed teeth** for catching and holding slippery fish. Their bodies were very streamlined, so they could slip through the water at high speed—like porpoises.

Like porpoises, ichthyosaurs gave birth to babies that were ready to swim and catch food as soon **as they were born.**

TYRANNOSAURUS

KRONOSAURUS

If you think Tyrannosaurus was frightening, just look at **Kronosaurus!** This giant pliosaur had a head that was **twice as large** as Tyrannosaurus—with twice as many **huge teeth!**

PLIOSAUR
(PLY-uh-sawr)

Different kinds of marine reptiles had **different kinds of teeth**—for catching and eating different kinds of prey. Pliosaurs like Krono-saurus had heavy teeth for **crushing shellfish.**

Plesiosaurs had long and pointed teeth for **grabbing slippery fish.**

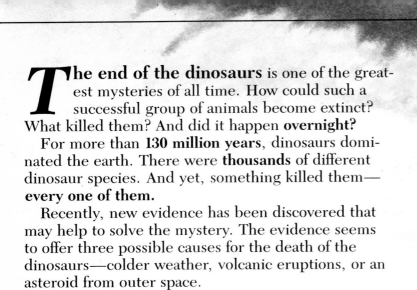

The end of the dinosaurs is one of the greatest mysteries of all time. How could such a successful group of animals become extinct? What killed them? And did it happen **overnight**?

For more than **130 million years**, dinosaurs dominated the earth. There were **thousands** of different dinosaur species. And yet, something killed them— **every one of them.**

Recently, new evidence has been discovered that may help to solve the mystery. The evidence seems to offer three possible causes for the death of the dinosaurs—colder weather, volcanic eruptions, or an asteroid from outer space.

VOLCANOES ERUPT

SUNLIGHT IS BLOCKED

If many volcanoes erupted at the same time a huge amount of smoke and ash would rise into the sky. This would **block out some of the sunlight.** If less sunlight could reach the earth's surface, the air would get **colder**. Colder air would weaken dinosaurs—and maybe kill some of them.

How could cold weather kill dinosaurs? Remember that cold-blooded reptiles need **heat from outside their bodies** to keep their bodies working. If they can't get enough heat from outside, they die.

If dinosaurs were **warm-blooded** like us, they could stand a small drop in the temperature. But **a large drop** would kill them, as it would kill us. Of course, we can put on clothes to keep warm—but dinosaurs didn't have overcoats!

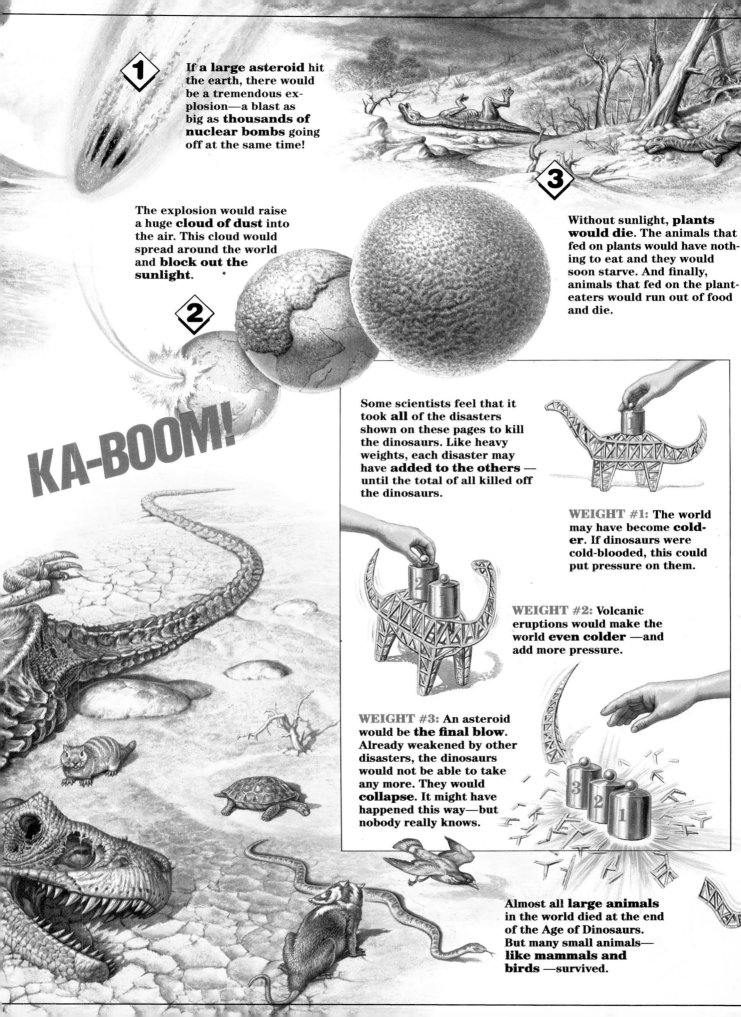

1 If **a large asteroid** hit the earth, there would be a tremendous explosion—a blast as big as **thousands of nuclear bombs** going off at the same time!

The explosion would raise a huge **cloud of dust** into the air. This cloud would spread around the world and **block out the sunlight**.

2

KA-BOOM!

3 Without sunlight, **plants would die**. The animals that fed on plants would have nothing to eat and they would soon starve. And finally, animals that fed on the plant-eaters would run out of food and die.

Some scientists feel that it took **all** of the disasters shown on these pages to kill the dinosaurs. Like heavy weights, each disaster may have **added to the others** — until the total of all killed off the dinosaurs.

WEIGHT #1: The world may have become **colder**. If dinosaurs were cold-blooded, this could put pressure on them.

WEIGHT #2: Volcanic eruptions would make the world **even colder** —and add more pressure.

WEIGHT #3: An asteroid would be **the final blow**. Already weakened by other disasters, the dinosaurs would not be able to take any more. They would **collapse**. It might have happened this way—but nobody really knows.

Almost all **large animals** in the world died at the end of the Age of Dinosaurs. But many small animals— like **mammals and birds** —survived.

REMEMBER:

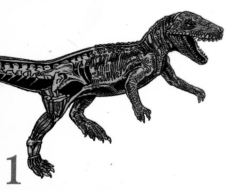

1
Dinosaurs were **the most successful group** of vertebrates that ever lived on earth. They "ruled the earth" for more than 130 million years. They were able to do this because they inherited **special advantages** from their ancestors, **the thecodonts**.

2
The legs of dinosaurs were under their bodies, so they could **run faster**. Legs under the body could also hold up greater weight—so dinosaurs could **grow larger**.

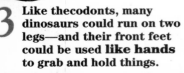

3
Like thecodonts, many dinosaurs could run on two legs—and their front feet could be used **like hands** to grab and hold things.

4
Dinosaurs inherited **socketed teeth** from thecodonts. Since these teeth were firmly anchored in the jaw, they were **stronger**.

5
Most meat-eating dinosaurs continued to run on two legs, and the **legs grew longer**. With longer legs, they could **run even faster**.

6
Tyrannosaurus rex and other large meat-eating dinosaurs had **expanding jaws**—So they could swallow large animals at **a single bite**.

7
Meat-eating dinosaurs had **serrations** on their teeth to help them cut up really big pieces of meat.

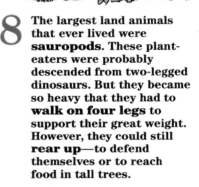

8
The largest land animals that ever lived were **sauropods**. These plant-eaters were probably descended from two-legged dinosaurs. But they became so heavy that they had to **walk on four legs** to support their great weight. However, they could still **rear up**—to defend themselves or to reach food in tall trees.

9
Sauropods may have grown so large as **protection from predators**. Or because larger bodies can **hold heat better**—so large reptiles could still move around when it was too cold for other reptiles to move.

NEW WORDS:

Sauropods
(SORE-uh-pods):
Dinosaurs that walked on four legs. They had long necks and tails—and some of them were the largest of all dinosaurs.

Ankylosaurs
(ann-KY-luh-sawrs):
Armored dinosaurs with armor plates **lying flat** on their backs. Ankylosaurs often had tails with clubs on the end to drive away predators.

Stegosaurs
(STEG-uh-sawrs):
Armored dinosaurs with a row of armor plates **standing up** on their backs. Stegosaurs also had spikes on their tails to help them defend themselves.

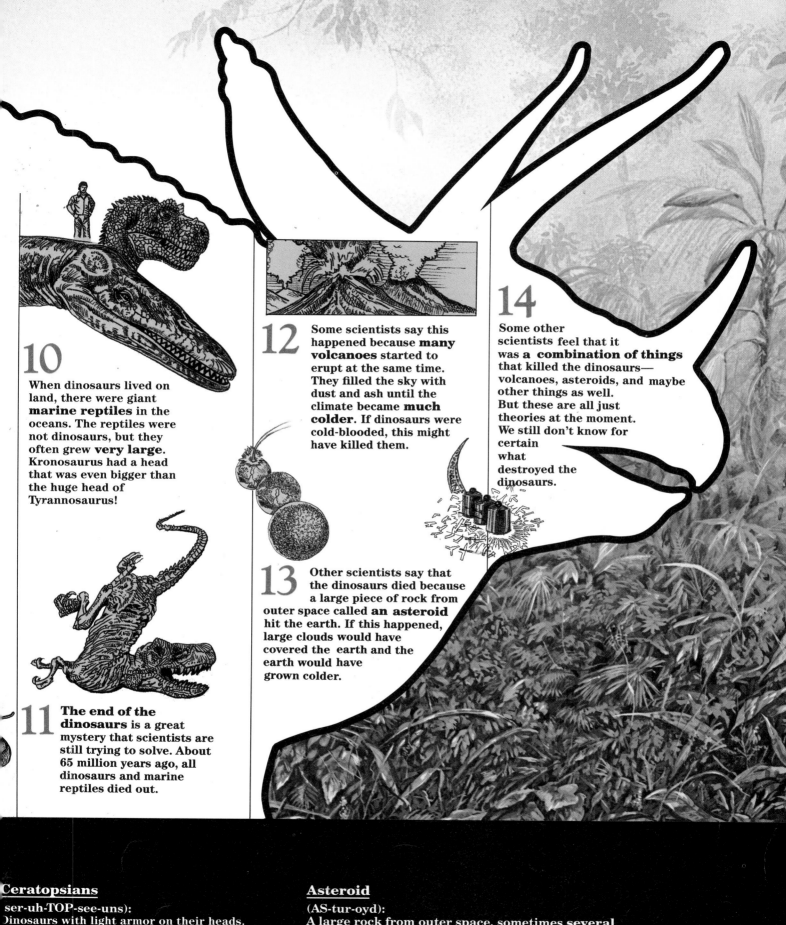

10

When dinosaurs lived on land, there were giant **marine reptiles** in the oceans. The reptiles were not dinosaurs, but they often grew **very large**. Kronosaurus had a head that was even bigger than the huge head of Tyrannosaurus!

11 The end of the dinosaurs is a great mystery that scientists are still trying to solve. About 65 million years ago, all dinosaurs and marine reptiles died out.

12 Some scientists say this happened because **many volcanoes** started to erupt at the same time. They filled the sky with dust and ash until the climate became **much colder**. If dinosaurs were cold-blooded, this might have killed them.

13 Other scientists say that the dinosaurs died because a large piece of rock from outer space called **an asteroid** hit the earth. If this happened, large clouds would have covered the earth and the earth would have grown colder.

14 Some other scientists feel that it was **a combination of things** that killed the dinosaurs—volcanoes, asteroids, and maybe other things as well. But these are all just theories at the moment. We still don't know for certain what destroyed the dinosaurs.

Ceratopsians

ser-uh-TOP-see-uns):
Dinosaurs with light armor on their heads.
They had **horns** and **strong beaks** to give
better protection.

Asteroid

(AS-tur-oyd):
A large rock from outer space, sometimes **several miles wide**. Some scientists think the dinosaurs died out because an asteroid struck the Earth.

Index

Acrocanthosaurus, 10
Age of Dinosaurs, 7
Allosaurus, 10, 15
Ankylosaurs, 12
Apatosaurus, 14
Armored dinosaurs, 8, 12-13
Armor plates, functions of, 12
Asteroids, as a reason for dinosaur
    extinction, 21

Beaks of dinosaurs, 13
Biggest dinosaurs, 14-15
Brachiosaurus, 17

Camarasaurus, 15
Carnivorous dinosaurs, 10.
    See also Meat-eating dinosaurs
Carnotaurus, 10
Centrosaurus, 13
Ceratopsians, 12
    horns and beaks of, 13
Cold weather, as a reason for
    dinosaur extinction, 20, 21

Daspletosaurus, 12-13
Dilophosaurus, 10
Diplodocus, 15, 17
Dromaeosaurus, 10

Eating style
    of meat-eating dinosaurs, 11
    of sauropods, 17
Edmontonia, 12
Euoplocephalus, 12
Evolution of dinosaurs, 7
Extinction of dinosaurs, 20-21

Flippers, of marine reptiles, 18

Food, of plant-eaters, 14

Gallimimus, 10

Hand structure, 9
    of marine reptiles, 18
Horns of dinosaurs, 13
Hypacrosaurus, 10

Ichthyosaur, 18

Kinds of dinosaurs, 7, 10, 12-13,
    14-15
Kronosaurus, 19

Leg structure, 8

Mamenchisaurus, 17
Marine reptiles, 18-19
Meat-eating dinosaurs, 10-11
    largest, 11
Mouths
    of meat-eaters, 11
    of plant-eaters, 17

Neck structure, 16

Offspring, of marine reptiles, 19
Ornithosuchus, 8

Plant-eating dinosaurs, 12-13
    reasons for large size of, 14
Plesiosaurs, 18-19
Pliosaurs, 18, 19
Predators, protection from, 14
Prey of dinosaurs, 10

Running ability, 10

Saichania, 12
Saltasaurus, 17
Sauropelta, 13
Sauropods, 14
    ancestors of, 15
Size, reasons for, 14, 15
Skeletal structure
    of sauropods, 16
    of thecodonts, 8
Spines, 12
Stegosaurs, 12
    tail spikes of, 13
Styracosaurus, 13
Supersaurus, 15
Survival success of dinosaurs, 8, 10

Tails
    of armored dinosaurs, 13
    structure of, 8
    as weapons, 13, 17
Teeth
    of marine reptiles, 19
    of sauropods, 17
    strength of, 9
    of Tyrannosaurus, 11
Thecodonts, 7, 8, 9
Torosaurus, 13
Tripod toe structure, 8
Tyrannosaurus, 10-11
Tyrannosaurus rex, 11

Velociraptor, 10
Volcanic eruptions, as a reason for
    dinosaur extinction, 20, 21

Walking style, 8
    of sauropods, 15